ADA COMMUNITY LIBRARY
10664 W. VICTORY ROAD
BOISE, ID 83709

D0820154

Demi Lovato

ABDO
Publishing Company

A Big Buddy Book
by **Sarah Tieck**

J
BIO
LOVATO

VISIT US AT
www.abdopublishing.com

Published by ABDO Publishing Company, 8000 West 78th Street, Edina, Minnesota 55439.

Copyright © 2010 by Abdo Consulting Group, Inc. International copyrights reserved in all countries. No part of this book may be reproduced in any form without written permission from the publisher. Buddy Books™ is a trademark and logo of ABDO Publishing Company.

Printed in the United States.

Coordinating Series Editor: Rochelle Baltzer
Contributing Editors: Heidi M.D. Elston, BreAnn Rumsch, Marcia Zappa
Graphic Design: Maria Hosley
Cover Photograph: *AP Photo*: Evans Ward/AP Images for Nickelodeon
Interior Photographs/Illustrations: *AP Photo*: Evan Agostini (p. 20), Kevin Ferguson (p. 23), Jennifer Graylock (p. 23), Donna McWilliam (pp. 11, 13), Chris Pizzello (p. 25), Dan Steinberg (pp. 5, 7), Mark J. Terrill (p. 8); *Getty Images*: Fred Duval/FilmMagic (p. 19), Demitrios Kambouris/WireImage (p. 10), Jeff Kravitz/FilmMagic (p. 23), Arnaldo Magnani (p. 7), K. Mazur/TCA 2008/WireImage (p. 27), Frank Micelotta (p. 28), Ethan Miller (p. 17), Tim Mosenfelder (p. 15), Andrew K. Walker (p. 15).

Library of Congress Cataloging-in-Publication Data

Tieck, Sarah, 1976-
  Demi Lovato : talented actress & singer / Sarah Tieck.
    p. cm. -- (Big buddy biographies)
  ISBN 978-1-60453-711-6
  1. Lovato, Demi, 1992---Juvenile literature. 2. Actors--United States--Biography--Juvenile literature. I. Title.
  PN2287.L656T54 2009
  791.4302'8092--dc22
  [B]
                                 2009015294

Manufactured with paper containing
at least 10% post-consumer waste

Contents

Rising Star

Demi Lovato is an actress and a singer. She has appeared in television shows and movies. Demi is known for starring in the movie *Camp Rock*. She has also **released** popular music.

Demi played Mitchie Torres in *Camp Rock.*

5

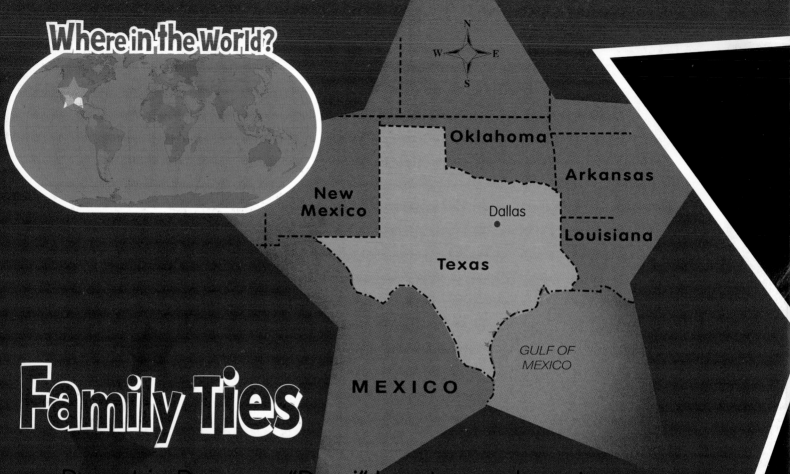

Family Ties

Demetria Devonne "Demi" Lovato was born in Dallas, Texas, on August 20, 1992.

Demi's parents are Patrick Lovato and Dianna Hart De La Garza. Demi also has a stepfather named Eddie De La Garza. Her older sister is Dallas Lovato. Her younger sister is Madison De La Garza.

Many of Demi's family members work in show business. Her mom (*above*) was once a singer and a Dallas Cowboys cheerleader. Demi's sister Madison (*right*) is an actress. And, her sister Dallas is a singer and an actress.

Demi has been homeschooled for part of her education. This means she learns from private teachers at home or on the road. Many young actors and singers are homeschooled.

Growing Up

Demi's parents divorced in 1994. Demi stayed in Dallas with her mother and older sister. She spent her childhood there.

Demi's father moved to New Mexico. He was unable to visit often. It was hard for them to stay connected.

A Young Actress

When Demi was growing up, Dianna sang country music. Demi says she got her voice from her talented mom.

Young Demi wanted to be a **professional** singer and actress. So, she **competed** in local and state **beauty pageants**.

She also **auditioned** for *Barney and Friends*. This is a popular children's television show. Demi was excited when she got a **role**!

Demi met actress Selena Gomez (*left*) at tryouts for *Barney and Friends*. They became friends right away.

Barney is a large purple dinosaur. His world is full of music, games, and fun.

Lights!
Camera! Action!

When she was six, Demi began to appear regularly on *Barney and Friends*. She played a girl named Angela.

Barney and Friends debuted in 1992. It has filmed for more than ten seasons. Many movies have been made, too.

Demi appeared on *Barney and Friends* for about two years. Around this time, she began to study music. She took singing lessons. She also learned piano, **guitar**, songwriting, and hip-hop dance.

Today, Demi often plays instruments as she sings.

Discovered

After leaving *Barney and Friends*, Demi had small roles on other television shows. In 2007, she appeared on Nickelodeon's *Just Jordan*.

Demi wanted to work for Disney. She auditioned for several roles. Finally, she got a part on *As the Bell Rings*. Demi played Charlotte on this popular comedy show.

Did you know...

Each episode of *As the Bell Rings* is about five minutes long. It is shown during breaks from regular shows.

Demi uses her singing and songwriting talent to boost her acting career. Her song "Shadow" was featured on *As the Bell Rings*.

Did you know...

The band members of Jonas Brothers acted in *Camp Rock*. Joe Jonas starred as Shane Gray, the lead singer of a band. Nick and Kevin Jonas played Shane's bandmates.

Big Break

People began to notice Demi's talent. She soon left *As the Bell Rings* for a bigger **role**.

In June 2008, Demi appeared in the Disney Channel's *Camp Rock*. It was her first starring movie role! Demi played Mitchie Torres, a poor girl who attends a music camp. Mitchie dreams of being a singer.

Demi's *Camp Rock* costars include Alyson Stoner and Kevin, Joe, and Nick (*left to right*) of Jonas Brothers.

Many fans love reading about the stars of *Camp Rock!*

Camp Rock is one of the Disney Channel's most successful movies. Almost 9 million people watched its debut!

The cast of *Camp Rock* has appeared in magazines and on television. Fans can purchase *Camp Rock* clothes, toys, books, albums, and DVDs.

Rock Star

In addition to her work as an actress, Demi shines as a singer. In summer 2008, she joined Jonas Brothers on their Burning Up Tour.

Then in September, Demi **released** her **debut** album. It is titled *Don't Forget*. The album became very popular with fans. Demi plans to record more albums in the **future**.

The Jonas Brothers tour was made into a 3-D movie. 3-D movies look as if they're coming off the screen.

Kelly Clarkson (*left*) is one of Demi's heroes. She inspired Demi (*above*) to be a better singer.

Did you know...

Demi sings the opening song of *Sonny with a Chance*. It is called "So Far So Great."

New Opportunities

After *Camp Rock*, Demi had many opportunities. In February 2009, she began starring in *Sonny with a Chance* on the Disney Channel. Her character's name is Sonny Munroe. In the show, Sonny moves to California to be an actress.

Demi's costars include Tiffany Thornton (*left*) and Sterling Knight (*right*). Tiffany and Sterling's characters compete with Sonny.

In June 2009, Demi starred with Selena Gomez in *Princess Protection Program*. Demi played Princess Rosalinda.

In the movie, Rosalinda's country is in danger. So, she is put in the Princess Protection Program. She pretends to be Rosie, a normal teenager. Rosie becomes friends with Carter, Selena's character.

Demi and Selena (*left*) were very excited to act together again. They are close friends.

In summer 2009, Demi headlined her first tour!

Did you know...

Headlining a tour is when a singer is the main act in a number of concerts. This is an important accomplishment for a singer!

Buzz

Demi continues to advance as an actress and a singer. In summer 2009, she headlined her first tour! And, she plans to work on *Camp Rock 2* with the Jonas Brothers band members. Fans are excited to see what's next for Demi Lovato. Many believe she has a bright future.

Snapshot

★ **Name**: Demetria Devonne "Demi" Lovato

★ **Birthday**: August 20, 1992

★ **Birthplace**: Dallas, Texas

★ **Appearances**: *Barney and Friends, Just Jordan, As the Bell Rings, Camp Rock, Sonny with a Chance, Princess Protection Program*

★ **Album**: *Don't Forget*

★ **Toured with**: Jonas Brothers

Important Words

audition (aw-DIH-shuhn) to give a trial performance showcasing personal talent as a musician, a singer, a dancer, or an actor.

beauty pageant (PA-juhnt) a contest between a group of girls or women that often includes a showing of beauty, talent, and character.

comedy a funny story.

compete to take part in a contest between two or more persons or groups.

debut (DAY-byoo) a first appearance.

future (FYOO-chuhr) a time that has not yet occurred.

guitar (guh-TAHR) a stringed musical instrument played by strumming.

professional (pruh-FEHSH-nuhl) working for money rather than for pleasure.

release to make available to the public.

role a part an actor plays in a show.

Web Sites

To learn more about Demi Lovato, visit ABDO Publishing Company online. Web sites about Demi Lovato are featured on our Book Links page. These links are routinely monitored and updated to provide the most current information available.

www.abdopublishing.com

Index